Roman Myths

Roman
Myths

Retold by Anthony Masters
Illustrated by Peter Dennis

MACDONALD YOUNG BOOKS

To Robina – the Light, A.M.

First published in Great Britain in 1999 by Macdonald Young Books,
an imprint of Wayland Publishers Limited
61 Western Road
Hove
East Sussex
BN3 1JD

Find Macdonald Young Books on the Internet at
http://www.myb.co.uk

© Macdonald Young Books 1999
Text © Anthony Masters 1999
Illustrations © Peter Dennis 1999

Editor: Lisa Edwards
Designer: Dalia Hartman

A CIP catalogue for this book is available from the British Library.

Printed and bound in Portugal by Edições ASA

ISBN 0 7500 2640 5

Contents

The Survivors

The hungry dogs were barking and growling, their bloodshot eyes glinting and their yellow fangs bared. For a moment Jupiter and his son, Mercury, stood still and faced the ferocious pack. How the gods wished that they weren't disguised as beggars.

'Don't be afraid,' said Jupiter. 'The villagers are bound to call them off.'

Mercury wasn't so sure. By now, the mangy dogs were leaping up at them, howling like wolves.

Jupiter and Mercury turned and ran, the dogs snapping and snarling close behind them, their fangs dripping saliva.

At last the gods outran the pack and stood gasping on a hilltop, looking down at the miserable rows of houses in the valley below. Their gaze fell on deserted streets, barred doors and hostile faces glaring out from dirty windows. This had been the most unwelcoming village of all.

Jupiter and Mercury had journeyed to Earth for a particular purpose. They and the other gods believed that the human race had become wicked and selfish and should be destroyed. So, disguised as beggars, the two immortals were searching the world for any decent, hospitable human beings who deserved to be saved. In their travels they had knocked on hundreds of doors, begging for food and drink, but so far they had only been set on by dogs.

As they rested for the night, they listened to the baying of the pack in the valley below. Grimly, Jupiter said to Mercury, 'It seems that we were right. The entire human race needs to be destroyed. So far, we have met nobody worth saving. The sooner Neptune opens the floodgates and drowns them all the better. It's nothing less than they deserve for being so selfish.'

'Let's try just once more, Father,' pleaded Mercury. 'Surely there must be some mortals who will welcome us?'

Reluctantly, Jupiter agreed that they would knock on one more door.

On a neighbouring hillside next morning, the gods knocked on the door of an old man, Philemon, and his wife, Baucis.

Immediately after he opened the door to the two shabby figures, Philemon welcomed them inside.

He stirred up the fire while Baucis prepared a meal, spreading the table with the food and drink that usually lasted them a whole week.

The meal was simple but delicious: vegetable soup, salt pork, cheese, olives, eggs, pickles, cherries, a honeycomb and a jug of home-made wine. As the gods ate and drank, Philemon noticed that the wine jug remained full, even after it had been emptied to the last drop.

Philemon nudged Baucis. She had also noticed the jug miraculously refilling itself. It was a terrible shock for them both to realize that they were in the presence of gods.

At once, Philemon and Baucis kneeled before Jupiter and Mercury, horrified that they had offered such plain food and drink to such great immortal beings.

First, the old couple begged Jupiter and Mercury's forgiveness. Then, still believing this was not enough, they decided to sacrifice their old goose, a faithful companion for many years. But they couldn't catch the terrified creature which eventually hid squawking behind the gods.

Jupiter rose to his feet and forbade them to sacrifice the goose.

'You love her dearly,' he said, 'and you have done enough to make us realize your worth.'

Suddenly, a roaring of water could be heard. Neptune, god of the sea, had opened the oceans' floodgates. Philemon and Baucis clung to one another in fear.

'Don't be afraid,' said Mercury. 'You are the only mortals who are going to survive the great flood.'

Hurriedly, the gods led the old couple to the top of the hill, from where they saw the most incredible sight. A great tidal wave was bearing down on the village in the valley and already men, women, children and dogs were running for their lives.

The wave arched and lashed at the fleeing figures. Soon nothing but raging water could be seen – and the very last dog on Earth sounded its very last bark. Slowly the flood rose, destroying everyone and everything in its merciless path.

Philemon and Baucis turned away in horror, but Jupiter told them to lift their eyes and look. To their amazement, they saw that their humble cottage was not only standing clear of the water but changing in the most miraculous way. The old corner posts had become stone columns, the dirt floors had changed into marble, ornate carvings and gold ornaments decorated the doors, and the straw thatch had been transformed into a gilded canopy. The cottage had become a magnificent temple.

Jupiter grasped the old couple's hands and said, 'You are the only survivors of this terrible flood because you gave us everything you had. We will grant you any wish you desire.'

Philemon and Baucis thought carefully and talked together for a long time. Then Philemon spoke, saying that all they both wanted was to remain together forever. If the gods would let them live out their lives as priest and guardian of the temple, they would be happy.

'I have another request,' he begged. 'Please don't let me live to see Baucis in her grave, nor be laid in mine by her.' Jupiter at once assured Philemon that his requests had been granted.

Hand in hand, Philemon and Baucis walked away down the hill to the temple surrounded by the vast ocean that had destroyed selfish humanity.

Philemon and Baucis spent the rest of their lives in great happiness as keepers of the temple, and when Death eventually came for them, they were waiting together at the bottom of the steps.

As Death approached, Philemon saw leaves starting to grow in his beloved Baucis's hair, gradually covering her body, and he felt a wave of panic. But he knew the gods wouldn't allow one of them to die before the other. When he felt the leaves sprouting in his own hair he sighed with relief.

Philemon and Baucis clasped their leafy hands together and as they bade each other farewell, bark grew over their mouths. Gradually, Baucis was transformed into a linden tree and Philemon an oak.

The trees stood side by side in front of the temple for hundreds of years. They became landmarks for travellers and a constant reminder that those who are good and unselfish receive the eternal reward of the gods.

Romulus and Remus

Something had caught the she-wolf's eye. As she watched, the flimsy little basket bobbed up and down on the fast-flowing River Tiber. As the current pushed it into the centre of the river, it threatened to capsize at any moment. Floating driftwood kept sending the little craft spinning out of control and a collision with a floating log made it tilt dangerously.

The she-wolf loped along the densely wooded bank and suddenly halted. She crouched, with ears flattened, alerted to the sound of a thin wailing. The cries were different from those of her cubs, but just as helpless. Slowly, she padded towards the river's edge as the basket bounced into the shallows.

• • •

The two babies were named Romulus and Remus, and they had been cast adrift by their wicked great-uncle Amulius who, with his brother Numitor, jointly ruled over the town of Alba Longa in Italy. The brothers had quarrelled and Amulius had imprisoned Numitor. Not only this, he had forced Numitor's daughter, Rhea Silvia, to become a vestal virgin so that she could never bear a child who might challenge him.

But the gods had other plans. One day, Rhea Silvia was walking along the banks of the Tiber when she encountered a beautiful young man. He was none other than Mars, the god of war. They fell in love and, as a result, Rhea Silvia gave birth to twin boys, Romulus and Remus.

Amulius was furious. Determined to wipe out any rivals to his throne, he ordered that Rhea should be buried alive, and her babies set adrift on the river. But the gods were still watching and the powerful god of the river floated the brothers to safety in their basket, landing them in the shade of a fig tree beside a small cave.

As the she-wolf padded towards the basket, Romulus and Remus stopped crying. Being so young and innocent, they were not in the least afraid of her sharp teeth and claws, but only murmured with contentment when she began to lick them gently with her rough tongue. Soon the babies fell asleep.

Later, when they woke and began to cry again, the protective she-wolf knew exactly what would quieten them. She had raised many litters over the years, and treated Romulus and Remus as just two more cubs who needed to be suckled and comforted.

The she-wolf cared for the boys until they were found one day by Faustulus, the royal shepherd of Alba Longa. He took them home, and with his wife Larentia, lovingly brought them up.

Many years went by. One morning, Romulus and Remus woke to find the sun shining so brightly through the cottage windows that the light was almost blinding.

The brothers ran to open the door and saw outside a figure surrounded by dazzling light. A voice spoke their names slowly and with great love, and when they asked who was there, the man replied that he was their father, and that they were his two much-loved sons. As they gazed up at him, the brothers were convinced that their father must be a god because of the brilliant light that radiated from him.

'I am, indeed, Mars, god of war,' said the figure and he began to tell the two boys the story of their birth. Then Mars told them, 'It is your duty, both of you, to take up arms against the evil Amulius and restore your grandfather Numitor to the throne.'

With these final words, he left. The shocked brothers had no idea what to do, for they knew they could never start a revolution on their own. Their neighbours were gentle shepherds and farmhands, not warriors.

Nevertheless, the brothers called a meeting and asked for help. At first, the country people were reluctant to become involved, but when the shepherds and farmhands heard how the river god had rescued the boys from the Tiber and how the she-wolf had looked after them, they knew the battle was god-given and willingly agreed to fight.

Armed only with staves and slings, the peasant army marched on Alba Longa, battling so savagely and with such passion that they soon overcame any resistance. They then hunted down Amulius, executed him and restored the wise law-maker Numitor to the throne.

From then on, life in Alba Longa became ordered and peaceful. Its citizens no longer fought among themselves, and the population increased until the town became so overcrowded that Romulus and Remus decided a new city must be built. As a permanent memorial to their past, the brothers chose the sacred site on the banks of the Tiber where the she-wolf had suckled them.

But founding the new city was a huge task and one that placed a great strain on the brothers' relationship.

One day, while Remus was out hunting, Romulus marked out the city boundaries by ploughing furrows to show where the walls could be built. But when Remus came home, he mocked the new 'walls', jumping over them and laughing, and doing his best to humiliate his once dearly loved brother.

Sadly, Romulus now realized that he and Remus were never going to be able to rule the city together. To his dismay, he also recognized that they were falling out over power, just as Amulius and Numitor had done. He decided they must find a peaceful solution.

'Let's consult the omens,' Romulus suggested. 'Then we can decide which one of us will rule.'

The brothers agreed to consult bird omens, and they divided the land into two, one side lucky, the other side unlucky.

Remus saw six vultures on the lucky side, Romulus saw twelve vultures on the unlucky side.

Unfortunately, they were left with a problem. Both Romulus and Remus had forgotten to establish which counted as the better omen: more birds on

the unlucky side or less birds on the lucky. Both decided that his was the winning side!

Each one argued his case fiercely, Remus taunting Romulus and goading him mercilessly until Romulus's anger spilled over and they began to fight.

The battle was bitter, except for a moment when, as they stared into each other's eyes, they almost came to a halt. Then Remus taunted his brother once again and, seizing the advantage, Romulus drove his sword into him.

Remus sank to the ground, his wound pouring blood, and Romulus gazed down in horror at what he had done. Kneeling by his brother's side, he pleaded with the gods, 'Save Remus. You must make him live again. Please save my dearest brother's life.'

But the gods were deaf to his pleading.

A still-grieving Romulus was made king of the new city which had been named Rome in his honour. But the city seemed doomed: no women were prepared to live there which meant that no children would be born. It was as if by killing his brother, Romulus had unleashed a curse against the city of Rome itself.

In a bid to save the city, Romulus visited each neighbouring town and village, inviting the inhabitants to a festival in honour of Neptune, the god of the sea. At the same time, he declared a sacred truce.

'Friends and enemies can come safely together now,' Romulus declared.

But he was lying.

Believing that a sacred truce would never be broken, hundreds of people – women and children as well as men – travelled to Rome for the festival. The largest group of all were the women of the nearby Sabine people.

During the festival, a number of races were to be run and everyone looked forward to the competition. Romulus, however, was deeply uneasy for he knew what was going to happen.

At the sound of a trumpet, the crowds hurried to watch the first race between some young Romans. But just as the contest was about to begin, the young Romans produced concealed weapons and kidnapped the Sabine women. They imprisoned them and forced themselves upon them to make

them bear their children. Romulus was deeply ashamed of his wicked plan, but knew he had to populate the new city somehow.

When the terrible news spread, the Sabine men attacked Rome repeatedly and war raged for many years.

Finally, the Sabine women decided they'd had enough of this war of power, betrayal and revenge, and so they came up with a plan.

At the height of the fighting, the women marched fearlessly shoulder to shoulder into the very midst of the battle, driving apart their Roman husbands and the Sabine men. Then they halted and made a declaration. Although they had been kidnapped and forced to bear the Romans' children against their will, they were prepared to remain in the city if the fighting stopped. Such was the women's bravery and so great was their resolution that the war came to an end and a permanent peace was made.

The curse on Romulus and his city had been lifted by the courage of the Sabine women, and he continued to rule over Rome for the next forty years.

The Broken Promise

Venus watched in wonder as Anchises walked out of the forest and along the dusty road. He was returning home after a morning swim in the dew pond. It was no wonder that Venus was entranced, for Anchises was the most handsome, most athletic, most striking young man she had ever seen. Venus, the goddess of beauty, was determined that somehow Anchises would fall in love with her.

To achieve this, Venus decided to disguise herself as a mortal princess – a high risk for a goddess to take. But her obsession with Anchises had blinded Venus to dangerous acts.

She waited for Anchises at the next bend, her heart thumping painfully.

Anchises was surprised to find a beautiful princess, looking lost and lonely, out on the dusty road. He asked her if she needed help.

Thinking quickly, Venus replied, 'I'm afraid I'm lost. I came out for a walk and now I can't find my way back.'

'Where is your house?' asked Anchises, and Venus thought quickly once more.

'I'm staying in a summer palace in the forest.' She paused. 'I'm afraid I can't remember the name.'

Anchises and Venus looked deeply into each other's eyes, and, such is the power of the gods, Anchises immediately fell in love with her. He gently guided Venus back into the forest and she led him down a series of mysterious paths until they came to a turreted palace. White swans glided majestically upon a moat which glinted darkly like green twilight – the whole scene had been specially created for the occasion by Venus's magic.

Anchises and Venus enjoyed a long and wonderful romance, and eventually the now mortal Venus discovered that she was going to have a baby.

When she broke the news to Anchises, Venus decided to reveal her true identity and told him that he was to tell no one, either now or when their baby was born. Venus warned Anchises that if he did start boasting about fathering the child of a goddess, then he would be severely punished by Jupiter, king of the gods.

Anchises agreed not to reveal the secret and had every intention of keeping his promise. He respected Venus not just as the woman he adored but also as the all-powerful goddess of love.

When Anchises first saw his newborn son, Aeneas, he was amazed and overawed, for the child had inherited not just his father's beauty but his mother's as well.

Aeneas was a true wonder to behold and crowds flocked to see the baby, gazing into his cradle and crying out their words of admiration.

'He has the beauty of the gods,' commented one admirer, and at this Anchises felt a pang of resentment. Because of his promise, the true identity of Aeneas's mother could never be revealed.

As the months passed, Anchises grew more and more frustrated. Keeping the secret close to his heart for so long made him feel as if he was carrying an increasingly heavy burden. Anchises longed desperately to blurt it all out – and eventually the longing became greater than the fear of Jupiter's punishment.

Finally, the wine at a local banquet loosened Anchises's tongue. As he gazed around drunkenly at the tables of chattering people, he knew that none of these boring mortals had the faintest idea that he possessed such an extraordinary secret.

An intense desire to stun them with his good fortune overwhelmed Anchises, and as he gazed into his wine glass a false confidence overcame him. It would be all right. He could admit his secret and nothing would happen to him. Venus only wanted to save her own face and, anyway, the gods would understand. Anchises was just a mortal and mortals shouldn't be expected to keep such important secrets.

Anchises refilled his glass, took a deep breath and stood on the table. The chattering died away as the diners recognized Anchises, the man who had fathered an incredibly beautiful son whose mother was rumoured to be a mysterious princess.

They gazed up at him curiously and a deep silence fell.

'I have a secret I wish to share,' Anchises cried out, his voice slurred. 'I just can't keep it to myself any longer.' He raised his glass, the wine spilling over the top. 'I propose a toast to Aeneas's mother. The mother of my child. Let us drink to – Venus, the goddess of love.'

The long silence was broken at last by gasps and cries of amazement and Anchises wondered whether they believed him or not. But it didn't really matter. At last, he had unburdened himself.

Then Aeneas heard a deep roaring sound coming from high above him. It was a roaring that was loud and menacing and terrifying to hear, as if a great storm had suddenly erupted.

As Anchises gazed up in terror, the ceiling shattered and a gigantic thunderbolt with a sharpened point shot towards him.

There was no time for pleading as Jupiter's weapon hit its target and pierced Anchises through the heart. But it didn't kill him. Instead, when he gazed down at his hands Anchises saw they were like thin, shaking claws. His empty wine glass dropped to the floor and Anchises fell gasping to his knees, but not before he had caught a glimpse of himself in a mirror.

Anchises saw a ravaged face with wrinkled flesh, rheumy eyes and a grey beard. His good looks had gone forever.

The diners rose to their feet in horror, staring at the old man huddled on his knees, his head clasped in his hands, weeping for the loss of his beauty.

The Battle for Rome

The situation seemed hopeless. The only barrier that lay between the invading Etruscan army and Rome was a bridge suspended above the River Tiber. Three Roman warriors, Horatius, Lartius and Herminius were stationed at the head of the bridge while, behind them, the Roman army tried desperately to hack away at the supports and bring down the whole structure into the fast-flowing river. It was the task of the three warriors to hold off the Etruscans until the Roman army had finished the job – and time was running out.

If the warriors could hold out, Rome had a chance of survival. Everything depended on how quickly the bridge could be demolished. Glancing behind him, Horatius saw that the Roman army were only halfway through their task.

Lars Porsena, the Etruscan commander, was deeply impressed by the heroism of the three young soldiers on the bridge.

He was reluctant to give the order to attack, and instead advanced towards them. 'Get out of our way,' he commanded.

But Horatius remained steadfast and simply raised his sword and Lars Porsena knew he could delay no longer. If his army didn't cross soon, the Romans would have demolished the bridge.

The three Roman warriors watched the Etruscan army line up. The only advantage for Horatius and his companions was the narrowness of the bridge, for there was only room for them to face three Etruscan soldiers at a time. Nevertheless, the task still seemed impossible, for even if they managed to kill the first three, they would be replaced immediately by another, fresher trio and then another. All the while, Horatius, Lartius and Herminius would become increasingly exhausted.

As he awaited the first attack, Horatius checked the progress of the Roman army with the commander in charge of the demolition. But the timbers of the bridge were tough and the advance was slow.

'May the gods be with you,' was all the commander could say.

Horatius looked up to the sky and prayed. The gods had to be with them, for there was no way they could survive without help.

The first wave of the attack came and Horatius, Lartius and Herminius fought the first three Etruscans with a desperate strength. Behind them, the Roman army worked with the same vigour.

The three Roman warriors soon killed their opponents, piercing their heavy armour with their swords, but were then immediately locked into combat with another three. Soon Horatius, Lartius and Herminius were exhausted, and although not one of them had yet been wounded, they knew they couldn't last out much longer. The deadly heat, the weight of their armour and the ceaseless ring of steel as they fought were draining all their strength.

'How much longer?' Horatius yelled over his shoulder. 'For the sake of the gods – how long?'

'Seconds now,' replied the Roman commander. 'Only seconds.'

But the seconds seemed like hours. Horatius felt himself weakening and knew neither he nor the others could hold out much longer. But somehow they fought on frantically, until a crunching, vibrating sound was heard and the bridge began to slowly collapse under their feet.

As the bridge's supports toppled, Horatius ordered his two comrades to jump across to the Roman side of the Tiber while he stayed to hold off the Etruscan soldiers. As the last timbers of the bridge fell, Horatius struck at his opponent, knocking him into the river.

Horatius stood alone on the bridge head while the rest of the structure

was swept away in the fast-flowing waters. He had no chance of rejoining the Roman army, and the Etruscans were standing before him.

'Give us your surrender,' shouted Lars Porsena.

Horatius glanced back to Rome and imagined he could see the white porch of his house glinting in the sun. There was only one way to escape. He must swim across the Tiber.

Imploring the gods to watch over him, Horatius leapt into the lashing torrent below.

The weight of his heavy armour pulled him under at once. The Etruscan and Roman armies, united in their respect for Horatius's bravery, watched in alarm when he didn't surface.

Then a spontaneous cheer was heard as he suddenly appeared. But Horatius heard nothing as he was swept along in the current's roar.

He struck out for the bank, struggling forward again, still weighed down by the crushing burden of his armour, his body sore and bruised.

For a long time, both the Etruscans and the Romans thought they had lost Horatius as he sank from sight once again. But his amazing resilience and his will to survive were strong and he emerged again to battle against the current. Heading downstream, he eventually struck out for the Roman bank.

At this, Horatius's comrades sank to their knees and prayed, while the Etruscans watched in respectful silence.

When he sank again, he disappeared for such a long time that a great groan of despair came from the Romans. But when he suddenly surfaced, the Romans knew their prayers had been answered. Horatius swam on, his strokes becoming more powerful. Cheering broke out on both sides of the Tiber as he neared the Roman jetty. Suddenly the cries grew louder and Horatius realized that he was being warned. A massive piece of timber had broken loose from the wrecked bridge and was twisting and turning on the current towards him.

Horatius dived as deep as he could and on looking up saw the dark shadow of the timber above him, like some terrible monster hunting for prey upon the surface of the torrent.

Horatius clawed his way up to the surface, his lungs at bursting point. As he emerged, a loud cheer burst from the armies massed on both sides of the river. With his last iota of strength, Horatius reached out for the Roman jetty and was dragged at last from the deadly grip of the raging Tiber.

Horatius, saviour of Rome, was carried through the gates of the city on the shoulders of a vast, cheering crowd.

When he had rested, he returned to the river. Kneeling on the bank, he thanked the river god for saving him and then began to walk slowly and painfully towards the Palatine Hill and the white porch of home.

The Romans rewarded Horatius twice over for his outstanding bravery. He was given a large tract of land and oxen so that he and his family would live well for the rest of their days and, furthermore, a magnificent statue of him was erected on the shores of the Tiber. This stood for many hundreds of years as a memorial to a brave and selfless man.

The Monster Child

The sky of the lifeless Earth was dark with whirling storm clouds. Lightning cracked, jagged and fearsome and there was a strong smell of sulphur. Chaos was coming, and with it the creation of mankind.

Chaos was a burning sphere of life, made of fire and light, that was hurtling through the planetary system, spinning in the heavens as it came.

The first life on planet Earth was brought by Chaos which crash-landed in a desert region, glowing red, gently cooling until the first of two beings emerged. This was Uranus, sometimes known as Father Sky.

For a while Uranus stood gazing at the vast scene of desolation around him. Although there were mountain ranges and valleys, plateaus and plains, dust and rock, the Earth at this time was as lifeless as the Moon. Uranus stretched out his hands and poured life-giving rain, watering the desert and gradually making the Earth green and fertile.

Uranus was not the only life-giver to emerge from Chaos. The other was Gaia, sometimes called Mother Earth, who also brought life. She created oceans and rivers, trees and plants, and creatures of all kinds to inhabit the newly fertile planet.

So far, only Good had touched Earth – but Evil wasn't far behind.

The next being to arrive was Hecate. Her destiny was to become ruler of the Underworld.

Unlike the life-givers who would live for ever, the mortals they created would eventually die and descend to the Underworld – a dark, shadowy land beneath the Earth.

There, Hecate would be the queen of ghosts, and roam round her domain, with a whip in her hand and a pack of ghosts screaming balefully at her heels.

Foolishly, Uranus fell in love with Hecate. He wanted to impress her with a gift, but knew that this had to be something extraordinary.

For a long time he wracked his brains. Then he had an inspired thought. He would present Hecate with a child, but a most unusual one.

Taking equal portions of earth, air, water and darkness, Uranus moulded them into a ball and threw his special gift through the crack in the Earth's crust that led to the Underworld.

As the ball rolled down into the Underworld, it changed shape and became a long pillar. As it turned over and over, the friction transformed it into a living creature. But what a creature it was! Uranus had created a monster.

Hecate, however, was delighted, and cradled the hideous thing in her arms, deeply grateful for such a wonderful gift.

She fed her monster son on live woodlice, warm lamb's blood and puppies' entrails. She decided to call her baby Janus.

Unfortunately, Janus was unhappy with his life in the Underworld. The howling of his mother's ghostly servants and the revolting food he was forced to eat made him long for freedom. He began to look for an opportunity to escape, which eventually came when his mother left him alone one day while she rounded up her ghosts.

Plunging into the freezing cold waters of the River Styx that flowed through the Underworld, Janus floated to the upper world, landing on the banks of the River Eridanus in Italy.

There, the warm sun and nurturing daylight made Janus grow – something he could never do in the gloom of the Underworld. Unfortunately, he still retained his monstrous shape, with far too many heads, legs and arms, ears, eyes and noses. To anyone except Hecate, Janus was absolutely hideous.

At first, unaware of his ugliness, he just lay in the sun on the river bank. But when a boy passing by saw Janus, he screamed aloud in terror and hid behind the nearest tree.

'What's the matter?' asked Janus uncertainly.

'You're a monster. A hideous monster,' cried the boy.

'Am I?' Janus was bewildered. 'Don't I look right?'

'Of course you don't,' said the terrified boy.

'How should I look?' asked Janus.

'Like me!' Then the boy fled without a backward glance and, as he ran, Janus studied him carefully. Looking down at himself he realized that he looked nothing at all like the boy. Nor did he look like anyone else he came across, all of whom ran from him, screaming with fear.

Deeply depressed, Janus went into hiding for over seven centuries, concealing himself in the deepest of dark woods so that no one would see him. But he grew so lonely that he almost longed for his demonic mother, Hecate.

One day, however, a young shepherd found Janus curled up in the forest, fast asleep under an oak tree. The shepherd boy stared down at his monstrous body, his curiosity overcoming his fear.

When Janus awoke, the two exchanged glances, but the shepherd boy didn't run away screaming.

'Why are you so different from me?' the boy asked.

'I don't know,' Janus replied miserably. 'I was made as a gift for Hecate.'

Hearing this, the shepherd boy froze, for Hecate was notorious on Earth and much feared. She was the goddess of black magic and would often emerge from the Underworld to lurk at midnight at lonely crossroads and lay in wait for mortals. People laid out offerings and sacrifices to her so that she would leave them alone.

'Everyone's too frightened to be friends with me,' added Janus sadly. 'I haven't spoken to a soul for years.'

The shepherd boy offered Janus his hand. 'I'll be your friend,' he said impulsively, touched by the monster's plight.

From that moment on, life changed for the better for Hecate's monster child. The shepherd boy's mother brought him food and drink, and soon other visitors arrived, convinced that if Janus was Hecate's son – and if he was truly magical – he needed to be worshipped as a god.

Although he didn't want to be worshipped, Janus needed friends, and he began to live in peace. At last he was accepted.

But his peace was soon to be shattered by a battle that broke out between the gods, the giant Titans, and their offspring for control over the Earth. At the height of the war, Saturn, who was Janus's half-brother and leader of the Titans, was forced to find shelter in Italy. Janus, of course, knew where his half-brother was hidden.

The gods, furious with the Italian people for sheltering their enemy, hurled thunderbolts at the country, killing hundreds. The attack, the gods stated, would be repeated if Saturn's hiding place was not revealed.

Janus, finding himself at last in a position of importance, suggested a compromise: if the gods promised to show mercy to Saturn, he would reveal his hiding place.

The bargain was agreed and Saturn was exiled to the Islands of the Blessed. However, Jupiter, king of the gods, decided that Janus should be punished for siding against the gods and protecting his half-brother.

Janus was desperately worried, fearing that he would be sent back to the Underworld and his mother Hecate. But Jupiter's punishment was in the form of a task for Janus. He made him a god, and sent him to Mount Olympus, the kingdom of the gods, where he became the doorkeeper of Heaven. This meant that Janus was in charge of the single moment of time when the old year dies and the new year is born.

To fulfil his new position, Janus became rooted to the spot like the pillar he once resembled, but now with only two heads. One face gazed rigidly ahead while the other stared fixedly behind.

Despite this huge responsibility, Janus quickly realized that his task was worthless. And sadly, what Janus had feared most had come true. He was alone again.

Mors

The Underworld was a shadowy land beneath the Earth. It was where every mortal went to when they were dead, either to lead a peaceful existence if they had been good, or to undergo unending punishment if they had not. They shared this dark region with a great many demons, giants and monsters who had either been dumped there or were guarding magical, often hideous creatures.

Dead souls were rowed across the River Styx by Charon, the ancient ferryman who took them to the judgement seat of Pluto, king of the Underworld. The fare for the crossing was a copper coin laid under the corpse's tongue or a coin placed on each eye, and the boat was as ancient as Charon himself.

Another inhabitant of the Underworld was a strange and eerie warrior called Mors, who was the child of Night and sister of Sleep. The messenger of Death, Mors's task was to collect unwilling mortals whose time on Earth was over and take them to the Underworld for judgement. She had no body, only a head, arms and legs. To cover up this deficiency, she wore a skeleton just as if it were a suit of clothes. Mors also carried a reaping hook to make a grab for any mortal intent on escaping her.

• • •

Antonius didn't want to die. He had a bad fever which had made him so ill

he could hardly breathe and he knew that it would soon be time for him to travel to the Underworld for judgement.

Although he was only in his thirties he had lived a bad life, murdering his brother in a fit of jealousy, robbing an old man of his savings, drunkenly running down a child in his chariot, and stealing a friend's wife.

But Antonius was arrogant enough to think he could cheat Death. He planned to disappear into the deepest, darkest forest he knew and hide. Surely even Mors wouldn't be able to find him there.

Antonius was equally sure that his fever was getting better. He was over the worst and he was sure he could survive. Yesterday, however, he had discovered that a set of numbers had been carved on his front door with a sharp knife: 37 years, 8 months, 3 days, 14 hours, 6 minutes and 12 seconds – almost his exact age. By his calculations, Death would come today, soon after lunch.

Still feverish but hopeful, Antonius hurried to the forest and took such a complicated route that he was sure Mors would never find him. He had brought with him some survival rations – wine, cheese, bread and water – all of which he hoped would keep him going until the deadline was exceeded and Mors had given up.

Finding the densest part of the forest, he painstakingly built a warm shelter of branches, interwoven with foliage. Exhausted, Antonius lay down, had some wine and food and drifted off to sleep.

He woke in terror, and gazing out saw that night had fallen. Realizing that the deadline had passed, Antonius felt a surge of triumph. Mors had clearly lost her way in the forest and had not been able to claim him. It was definitely too late for her to bring him to judgement now, he decided. His fever had lifted and he was almost well again.

Just to be on the safe side, Antonius lay in his shelter for the next two days, using up all his supplies. He became increasingly optimistic. His life was not to be cut short after all. He had cheated Death.

The next day snow fell and Antonius decided to return home. He began to trek through the forest, which was vast and full of silence under its thick, white blanket of fresh snow. At first he was worried about leaving a trail of footprints but then he dismissed the danger. Mors came from the Underworld and was supernatural. If she had really been determined to find him, she would have done so.

It was only when he found he had returned to his own footprints in the snow that Antonius realized he was lost. At first he was merely impatient, but when he came back to them again – and again – he fell into a panic. Antonius was freezing cold, he had no food left and he was sure that his fever was returning.

Eventually, after retracing his own steps many times and with each snowbound glade and path looking exactly the same, Antonius felt himself completely defeated. Night came and he lay down. The softness of the snow comforted him and the return of his fever made him feel confused and unreal. Suddenly Antonius woke with a start.

The glade in which he was lying was lit by an unearthly light and he

saw a skeleton with a woman's head and limbs travelling towards him, hovering over the snow. She was smiling bleakly as Antonius tried to stagger to his feet.

'Are you Death?' he asked shakily.

Mors shook her head, 'I'm Death's messenger.' She was holding a reaping hook. 'As you know, I seek out those who try to cheat Death. You are overdue in the Underworld.'

Somehow Antonius dragged himself to his feet and began to run through the trees. He came to a wooded hill, and looking down into the valley below saw a river with a boat rowed by a hooded ferryman.

Sensing danger, Antonius turned away, but then he heard a rushing sound above him, like an arrow in flight. It was the reaping hook flying through the air. Antonius tried to dodge, but the hook's course was unerring, eventually lodging in the back of his tunic.

Mors came through the trees and took his hand in an icy grip.

'Is that the River Styx down there?' Antonius asked fearfully.

She nodded.

'And that's where you're going to take me?'

'You can't cheat Death,' Mors replied. She began to lead Antonius down the hill and through the trees to where the dark water glinted. He followed her obediently, knowing that all his efforts had been in vain. . .

Pomona

Vertumnus, god of the orchards, hid behind a tree, wondering how he could make Pomona notice him. Although he was a god, he hadn't the courage to approach her and start a conversation. He lost his nerve each time he tried. Worse than this, he also realized that if Pomona caught him hiding in her orchard she would order him out and tell him never to return.

Pomona only seemed interested in tending her apple trees, a virtue which Vertumnus, and her numerous other suitors considered a waste of her ravishing beauty.

Eventually, in desperation, Vertumnus went to Pales, the goddess of pastures for advice. She told him to remember his greatest skill, 'Each autumn your duty is to turn the leaves on the trees from green to gold and make sure they float down to the ground, leaving the branches bare so that in the spring new leaves will be able to grow in their place.'

'That's true,' replied Vertumnus impatiently. 'But what has that got to do with Pomona?'

'Everything,' said Pales. 'You can change the leaves from green to gold, so why don't you change yourself – from shy to bold?'

Vertumnus, however, wasn't in the least bold and he knew that such a transformation would be impossible. So he hit on another plan. Why not change the way he looked? Why not wear a disguise?

Pomona was a wood nymph and like all wood nymphs she thought about very little. Rivers, seas or mountains did not interest her. Nor did falling in love.

Her one passion was for her apple trees. Armed with a knife, Pomona would concentrate on pruning, thinning out the clusters of fruit so that the apples weren't spoilt by growing too densely together, and cutting the branches of the trees with great care so they didn't straggle.

She had never met Venus, the goddess of love, and because of this she had never found men attractive. In fact, she was afraid of their advances.

Pomona had already had problems with Pan who was one of the most persistent of her suitors. He was the god of shepherds and flocks and was always trying to entice her away from the orchard. Pomona had rebuffed him, but he made her feel uneasy, especially as her only protection was her trusty pruning knife and Pan was not put off easily. Recently, she had spotted him watching her again, hoping to catch her off guard.

Pan looked like a man from the waist up, but he had the ears and horns of a goat. From the waist down he had a goat's body. Pomona was disgusted by him, despite the fact that he played his pipes so beautifully for her.

Thoroughly irritated by her indifference, Pan would sometimes give his famous earsplitting cry. It was so piercing that it had been known to split a castle in two and send whole armies into retreat.

But although his shouting was trying, the noise never harmed Pomona, for the loyal apple trees rustled mockingly, deflecting the terrible sound. They weren't afraid of Pan even if Pomona was.

'Go away,' she would yell, her voice shaking, but Pan would only roar louder. Immediately the trees would rustle fiercely, as if a gale was blowing through their branches. Pan would laugh, enjoying the competition.

Whenever this happened, Pomona watched warily as Pan ran gleefully back to the woods and water meadows that were his home. There he was greeted by his subjects, the satyrs, who were also half human and half goat.

Vertumnus considered Pan's methods crude and set out not to make the same mistakes. His first disguise was that of a reaper, someone who was a gentle lover of nature. Wearing a belt of twisted hay, Vertumnus brought

Pomona corn laid in an elegant basket.

But Pomona ignored him.

Undeterred, Vertumnus tried out another disguise, appearing as a rugged ploughman.

But Pomona still ignored him.

Vertumnus began to panic and assumed an assortment of disguises in quick succession. He appeared as a vine tender, and when this didn't work, he reappeared disguised as an apple gatherer, and then a soldier, a fisherman and finally a bee keeper.

But Pomona ignored all of them.

Miserably, Vertumnus racked his brains. Then he had an inspiration. If Pomona was determined to ignore men, he would disguise himself as a sweet, grey-haired old lady. This time the disguise worked and Pomona welcomed her visitor. Admiring the fruit, the disguised Vertumnus began to talk to Pomona.

'What a hard worker you are, my dear,' said the old lady, and placed a very masculine kiss hard on Pomona's lips. Pomona didn't respond, but at least she didn't order the old lady away. Taking heart, Vertumnus sat on a bank and said in a quavering voice, 'If that tree stood alone and had no vine clinging to it, there would only be useless leaves. Because they're together they've both achieved a good deal more.'

But this heavy hint was lost on Pomona who had already returned to her pruning.

Vertumnus spoke again, and this time his voice was more strident, 'If the vine wasn't twisted round the elm, it would simply lie on the ground and bear no fruit.'

Pomona still paid no attention.

'Why don't you take a lesson from the tree and the vine? Why don't you unite yourself with someone?' Vertumnus's voice was even more strident now and sounded most unlike the old lady he was meant to be.

'I don't have to,' Pomona yawned, still snipping away. 'I've got my fruit. Why should I want anything else?'

Vertumnus, however, was determined not to give up, for he might

never get another opportunity. Conscious that he was taking an enormous risk, he pleaded, 'Why don't you let an old woman give you some advice? Accept Vertumnus as your suitor. I know him as well as I know myself. He loves you and you alone – not like Pan and your other suitors who will look at anyone. He's young and handsome and, of course, he's an expert at disguise. You've got a lot in common. He loves apple trees too.'

But Pomona only shrugged and yawned.

In desperation, Vertumnus decided to tell Pomona the tale of Iphis and Anaxarete as a warning of where her indifference would lead:

'Iphis was a young man of humble background who had fallen in love with Anaxarete, the daughter of a noble. He knew from the start that he had little chance of being accepted as a suitor, but he was so obsessed with her that he arrived at Anaxarete's house begging her servants to speak up for him. When they refused to help, he decided to write loving messages on tablets of stone and hang garlands of flowers on her gate. But when she received the tablets and saw the garlands, Anaxarete only mocked Iphis.

'Utterly humiliated, Iphis fastened a rope to the gatepost and cried out, "Here's one garland that should please you then!"

'Iphis hanged himself and was eventually carried home to his mother by Anaxarete's servants.

'Some days later, Iphis's funeral procession passed Anaxarete's gate, and hearing the weeping of the mourners she ran to her window.

'Directly she saw Iphis's corpse, Anaxarete began to stiffen, and soon she couldn't move. Her limbs became as stony as her cold heart.

'Still staring out of the window, she turned into a statue. When it was discovered, Anaxarete's rigid body was moved to the Temple of Venus where it still stands today.'

When Vertumnus had finished his tragic story, he saw that the tale hadn't had the slightest effect on Pomona, who was concentrating on a particularly difficult piece of pruning. She didn't even turn round but kept snipping away with her scissors.

Feeling as rejected as Iphis, Vertumnus got up, ripped off his disguise and walked out of the orchard. At the gate he turned back, half wondering whether to hang himself too.

Then, to his amazement, he saw that Pomona had turned towards him at last, and their eyes met.

She seemed bewildered. The old woman had gone and for the first time Pomona was seeing Vertumnus as himself.

'You're beautiful,' she said quietly.

'More beautiful than an apple tree?'

'Far more beautiful than an apple tree,' Pomona replied.

She ran towards him, arms outstretched, and Vertumnus did the same. They met in the centre of the orchard as the leaves rustled around them.

Vertumnus and Pomona spent the rest of their lives together, working in the orchard, harvesting the apples and tending the trees.

The Deadly Cave

The traveller had come far, heading across country on a journey to see his brother who was a rich man. This summer, heavy rain had made his crops fail and he needed a loan or, better still, a gift to make up for what he had lost.

The traveller had already walked many miles and was exhausted, and although he had intended to press on through the night he lay down by the River Tiber and slept heavily. But just after midnight he woke, conscious of a huge shadow blotting out the face of the moon. The traveller sat up, staring ahead, unable to make out what it was. The thing moved and he screamed again and again.

Down in the nearby village, the traveller's screams were heard, but the inhabitants turned over in their beds and the children buried their faces in their pillows. They had heard screaming many times before and each of them knew all too well what was causing the terrible outcry.

Meanwhile, the traveller was facing something so hideous that his screams eventually stuck in his throat and he simply gazed numbly at the monstrous thing whose vile jaws were now bathed in the light of the full moon.

• • •

The cave by the Tiber was deeply feared by local people. Only some unwary traveller, or an equally unwary animal, would go anywhere near the dreadful place, especially at night.

For in the cave lived Cacus who was the son of Vulcan, the blacksmith god, and Medusa whose gaze turned all who looked at her to stone. Cacus was a monster with the body of a huge spider, limbs like saplings and with three fire-breathing heads on a single neck.

Hating the sun, Cacus hid all day in the cave and hunted at night, preying on anything warm-blooded that crossed his path. Owls, cattle, wolves, lions and human beings were all among his victims. As a symbol of power, Cacus spiked his victims' heads like totems on the banks of the river. The traveller had joined the totems now, his mouth open in a soundless scream.

• • •

Cacus's reign of terror continued unchecked for many years until the great hero Hercules arrived.

Hercules was the child of a relationship between Jupiter, king of the gods, and the mortal queen Alcmena. Knowing that the baby would be hated by his jealous wife Juno, Jupiter had ordered Mercury, messenger of the gods, to bring the newborn baby to Juno secretly by night so that it could feed from her breast.

When she discovered how she had been used, Juno was furious, but it was too late. The secret that Jupiter had kept from her for nine months was out. Not only had she been betrayed by her husband's faithlessness but because the baby had been fed on a goddess's milk, Juno had unwittingly given the child immortality.

Unable to destroy Hercules, Juno nevertheless launched a series of attacks on him, eventually managing to drive him to a moment of madness in which he killed his wife and children in the most appalling massacre. As a result of this crime, the gods decreed that Hercules had to be punished by being given a set of apparently impossible tasks. But Hercules had at least some chance of succeeding because he happened to be immortal. After skinning the Nemean lion, killing the Hydra, catching the Keryneian hind, executing the Erymanthian boar, cleaning the Augean stables, driving out the Stymphalian birds, taming the Cretan bull, taking Diomedes's flesh-eating horses and stealing the golden belt of Hippolyta, Hercules also had to face stealing cattle from the island of the giant Geryon. But like the other labours, he managed to accomplish this, driving the herd through Italy.

It was unfortunate, however, that Hercules stopped to let the cattle drink from the River Tiber, not far from Cacus's grisly cave. It was getting dark so he decided to let them rest there for the night, eventually falling asleep himself.

Cacus couldn't believe his good fortune, and that night the monster seized four bulls and four heifers,

covering up their tracks so that Hercules wouldn't come after him – or so he hoped. Even Cacus had heard of Hercules's exploits, and knowing he was immortal feared him greatly. But the monster's hunger for blood and flesh overrode his caution; he couldn't resist the giant's cattle.

Hercules woke next morning and, not bothering to do a head-count, began to round the beasts up and drive them on.

Now that it was daylight, Cacus was asleep and sated, having eaten the four bulls and three of the heifers. But he had not been able to manage the final heifer and as the rest of the herd passed the cave she began to low and the beasts bellowed in reply.

Hercules raced towards the dark mouth of the cave which he found blocked by a huge boulder that even he couldn't shift. Then, to his horror, he saw the totem heads gazing sightlessly ahead as vultures wheeled around them. Using his anger to increase his strength, Hercules grabbed a piece of jutting rock on which vultures often waited for scraps of flesh, wrenched it sideways and tore the cliff apart. For a moment he stood waiting, but nothing emerged from the cave except the foulest stench he had ever smelt.

He forced himself to peer inside, gazing at the monstrous Cacus as his three heads belched flame. Hercules shuddered, for he had never seen such carnage. Summoning up his courage, he jumped down from the rock into the cave and stood before the fire-breathing monster with its hideous spider's body.

Ducking under the flames, Hercules reached up for Cacus's neck and quickly tied the dark flesh into a knot.

Standing back, he watched the monster choke to death. Hercules then dragged Cacus out of the cave to wither away in the sunlight.

Leading the surviving heifer back to the herd, Hercules passed a small group of local people who had come to see for themselves that the spider monster was well and truly dead.

As the sun rose high in the noonday sky the terrible creature's flesh continued to wither until there was nothing left of Cacus but dust. A great shout of triumph came from the crowd as they took the grisly totem heads and threw them into the fast-flowing Tiber.

The Evil Woods

Octavia ran like the wind towards the dark green woods, determined to annoy Larius, her lover. She wanted to punish him for the way he had quarrelled with her as they picnicked on the top of the hill.

In the valley below, the woods whispered quietly in the breeze.

'Don't follow me,' Octavia shouted over her shoulder. 'I never want to see you again.'

'I wouldn't dream of following you,' Larius yelled back. 'In fact, I'll leave you well alone until you come to your senses.'

At this, Octavia's heart filled with fury, for in running away she hoped to persuade Larius to follow her. She was afraid he was growing tired of her, and she wanted to test him out. But so far, the test was working against her. And the woods that had looked sinister enough from the top of the hill, now looked positively evil.

For a moment, Octavia hesitated. The breeze had dropped and the world was still. Deathly still. The sun was burning hot and, although the woods were shady, they appeared dank and gloomy and unwelcoming.

Perhaps she should swallow her pride and turn round and go back to Larius? She had been too distrustful – of course he only had eyes for her. But Octavia had convinced herself that she'd seen him gazing at Camilla. There could be no doubt that he was being unfaithful to her. No doubt at all.

She would hide in the woods, and if Larius loved her he would come looking for her. Octavia brushed aside the dusty green leaves and pushed her way in. Cobwebs hung from branches and her feet trod upon smooth, slippery moss. There were patches of bog seeping through the unnaturally bright-green grass.

Octavia was entering a different world where the sun didn't penetrate and a green gloom hung beneath the canopy of tree tops. The dampness seemed to force itself into her throat, making her breathing uncomfortably fast and shallow. Eventually, she came to a halt, certain that the forest would go on for ever and that she would never find her way through.

A wave of panic engulfed Octavia as she gazed around. She realized that the trees all looked the same and showed no sign of thinning out. Then her foot sank into squelching moss and she smelt a strong whiff of sulphur.

'Excuse me.' Although the voice was low and polite and reassuring, Octavia whipped round with a whimper of fear.

'Who is it?' she cried, unable to see any one at all in the deep gloom.

The bushes parted and a handsome young man came towards her. He was short in stature and his eyes were dark and shining.

'I'm sorry if I frightened you. Are you lost?'

Octavia nodded.

'Then I think I can help you.'

'Who are you?' Octavia asked suspiciously.

'I'm Faunus, god of trees and pastures.'

She was immediately worried. 'But I'm just a mortal.'

'And you are in my kingdom,' said Faunus.

Octavia sank down on her knees before Faunus, completely overawed. 'Am I trespassing?' she asked nervously.

'Not at all.'

'Will you help me find a way out?'

'Of course, but I'd like to show you a little hospitality first.'

Octavia smiled at him gratefully. She had recovered her confidence and was looking forward to telling Larius all about her encounter with this handsome young god – a meeting that would surely make him jealous.

'This way,' said Faunus, pushing aside some branches. To Octavia's amazement, a clear, straight path stretched before them.

'Where are we going?' she asked, suddenly fearful.

'Just to see a little spectacle I've arranged.'

'What kind of spectacle?'

'A sacrifice actually,' Faunus grinned at her cheerfully. 'I think you'll find it fun.'

Octavia cheered up. She'd seen quite a few sacrifices already for they were a popular form of entertainment in Rome.

Faunus and Octavia walked along the path until they reached a glade in which a large altar stood. But the altar was bare and there was no sign of any sacrifice.

'Where is the victim?' asked Octavia.

'She'll be here soon,' Faunus said in a matter-of-fact voice. He picked up an axe lying beside the altar and began to sharpen it.

'She?' asked Octavia. 'Do you mean a female lamb?'

'No, we're sacrificing a human being today.'

'Who is it?'

'A young girl.'

'Who is she being sacrificed to?'

'To my father, Mercury.'

'Oh…' Octavia gazed around the glade, but there was no sign of an audience or the victim. She began to feel a little uneasy. 'When will this girl be here?' she asked.

'She's late,' said Faunus, a little testily. 'So, would you grant me a favour?'

'What's that?' asked Octavia, anxiously.

'Just put your head on the altar so I can see where the axe might fall.'

Octavia hesitated nervously.

'Then, when we've completed the sacrifice I'll show you safely out of the wood.'

Faunus grinned again. He had a nice, reassuring sort of grin.

'Very well,' Octavia agreed, and she went across and placed her head on the altar. 'Is this all right?'

'Just move a little to the left.'

Octavia obeyed.

'Now a little to the right.'

She obeyed him again. She could hear Faunus standing behind her, breathing heavily.

Octavia waited patiently, unaware that he had raised the axe. He brought the blade down very precisely and Octavia's head rolled across the altar and on to the mossy ground.

'The sacrifice,' said Faunus quietly, 'is complete.'

But the gods were displeased with Faunus. He had played his tricks once too often. Again and again, he had pretended to welcome young men and women to his kingdom – and then sacrificed them to Mercury.

The gods had warned that if this happened again Faunus would be severely punished, and this time there would be no mercy. As a punishment for Octavia's sacrifice, the gods gave Faunus a goat's hindquarters, pointed ears and horns, and imprisoned him in the woods for eternity. And this is where he and his descendants, the Fauns, have lived ever since.

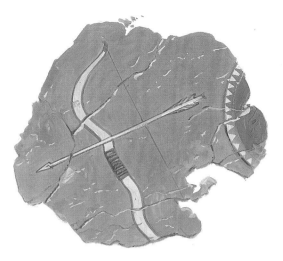

Cupid and Psyche

'Of course I am the most beautiful woman in the world,' said Psyche. 'In fact, I'm even more beautiful than Venus, the goddess of love.'

This was a fatal boast, but Psyche, the youngest and most beautiful daughter of the king and queen of Sicily, wasn't very worldly-wise. Nevertheless, suitors flocked to the palace, all anxious to marry her.

Furious at her vanity, Venus decided to teach Psyche a lesson. She ordered her son, the winged god of love, Cupid, to transfix the princess with an arrow of desire which would make Psyche fall in love with the first person her eyes alighted on.

Venus had not considered the possibility that Cupid himself might fall in love with Psyche. And the moment he saw her he was enthralled by her beauty. Ignoring his mother's commands, he spirited her away to a secret palace hidden in a valley of flowers and surrounded by needle-sharp peaks, without telling her who he was – or letting Psyche catch sight of his face. Each day invisible servants saw to Psyche's every whim and wish, and every night Cupid came to her room. But there was a catch, for Cupid told Psyche that if she ever looked directly at him, she would die.

Psyche soon grew deeply lonely and asked if her sisters could come and visit. Cupid agreed, commanding the west wind to carry them to her.

Their reunion was joyful but Psyche's sisters couldn't understand why she had never seen her lover. They told her that the reason he had insisted that she should never look at him must be because he was a monster.

Psyche was very worried, especially when her sisters gave her a knife and a lamp, and told her to light the lamp and use the knife to kill the monster.

At first she tried to banish the doubts they had planted in her mind, but eventually Psyche could bear it no longer, and when Cupid was asleep, she lit the lamp. Overwhelmed with relief at his beauty, her hand shook and a drop of burning oil from her lamp scalded his shoulder. As Cupid woke with a cry of pain, Psyche fainted with fear.

When she woke she found herself in a desolate country she had never seen before. The palace, the flower gardens and Cupid had completely vanished.

Psyche wandered about, miserably pleading for help from anyone she met, but no one was prepared to come to her aid. Ceres, goddess of the Earth, said she was not allowed to interfere in lovers' quarrels, and Pan, god of flocks and shepherds, was just as unhelpful.

'I only understand sheep and goats,' he told Psyche. 'I don't understand people and their ways.'

Finally, she returned to Ceres and pleaded again, and in exasperation Ceres gave Psyche some advice, 'You're worthy of our pity, but I can't shield you from Venus's anger. You'll have to go to her and beg forgiveness.'

Psyche went to the Temple of Venus and humbly said how sorry she was to have boasted that she was more beautiful than the goddess.

But Venus was not able to forgive so quickly and told Psyche she would have to undergo a series of impossible tasks.

'This is the first,' said Venus grimly, leading Psyche into a barn that was filled with unsorted millet, barley and wheat grains. 'I want you to sort these out into three neat piles,' she ordered briskly.

'By when?' gasped Psyche. The job looked as though it might last her entire lifetime.

'By morning,' said Venus with a triumphant smile, and returned to her temple.

Psyche sat down and wept. Ceres heard her crying and hurried into the store to see what was happening. When she heard Psyche's woeful tale, Ceres went to an ant heap and commanded its busy residents to come and help Psyche. Scurrying about the floor of the barn, the ants soon had the millet, barley and wheat sorted into three separate piles. Psyche was delighted and grateful.

But when Venus arrived in the morning she was furious, for she realized that no human being could ever have achieved such an impossible task.

'You wicked girl,' she shouted. 'You were helped to do this, weren't you?'

Psyche simply hung her head.

'You're not only vain, but you're stupid too if you thought you could deceive me.'

Psyche said nothing and Venus flung her a slice of black bread for her breakfast.

'I'm going to give you another task. You're to go through the grove and down to the meadow by the river. There you will find a ram with a golden fleece. You must catch the ram, pluck its wool and weave me a head-dress by this evening.'

'Impossible!' cried Psyche.

'That's true,' observed Venus as she returned once again to her temple.

Psyche wandered down to the meadow and stood watching the golden ram who looked extremely aggressive. She knew she would never be able to catch him, let alone pluck his wool.

Then she felt a tap on her shoulder and saw that Pan had crept up behind her.

'You look sad,' he said. 'Is there another problem, Psyche?'

Once again she began to weep as she told Pan the next impossible task Venus had presented her with.

'I can solve that,' he said unexpectedly, and she gazed at him in amazement.

'You wouldn't help me when I asked you before,' she whispered. 'Anyway, Venus will only find out.'

Pan grinned at her, 'What else can she possibly do to you?'

So when the noonday sun had driven the sheep into the shade and they had begun to sleep, Pan and Psyche went to the meadow and gathered the

golden wool that had got caught up in the hedges and trees. Then Pan showed Psyche how to plait the wool into a head-dress.

She returned to Venus, her mission complete, but Venus was even more furious than before.

'You couldn't have done this!' she shouted.

'But I did,' Psyche stuttered.

'Liar. Now I have another task for you and it's a task for which you can't possibly find any help.'

When Psyche heard what the task was she went cold with fear. She had to take a box to Proserpina, who for six months of the year lived in the Underworld as Pluto's queen. The remaining six months she lived in the upper world of the living, where she brought spring and summer to Earth. The stress of tending Cupid, who was ill from the lamp-oil burn, had made Venus lose some of her beauty and she wanted Proserpina to send a little of her own loveliness to replace the loss.

Very few mortals had ever succeeded in journeying to the Underworld and returning. Nevertheless, Psyche knew she had to make the attempt.

As she began to descend towards Charon, the ferryman who rowed the dead over the River Styx into the Underworld, an unseen voice boomed out from a tower. It told her there was a secret entrance to the Underworld through a cave. If she took this route she would avoid most of the immediate dangers, including Charon who would definitely refuse to row her back to the upper world.

'When Proserpina has given you the box filled with her beauty,' the voice warned, 'you must make sure you never look inside it.'

Psyche eventually reached the Underworld, using the cave as a back door and arrived safely at Proserpina's palace. She delivered the message from Venus and the box was soon returned to her, then Psyche hurried back to the cave, conscious of the souls in torment around her.

Her mission accomplished, Psyche at last reached the upper world again, but a terrible longing had possessed her and it refused to go away. She simply had to open the box and examine the beauty that lay inside.

At the back of her mind, Psyche also wondered if she might borrow some of it, for she hadn't lost her love for Cupid and was anxious to return to his side and win back his love.

She carefully opened the box but it was not beauty that lay inside.

Instead, it contained a portion of deadly deep sleep from the Underworld, and Psyche immediately fell down unconscious on the path.

Cupid, whose wound had been healed by none other than Jupiter, king of the gods, came to Psyche's rescue. He gathered up the deadly sleep from her body, returned it to the box and then wakened his beloved with a light touch from one of his arrows.

'You are too vain,' Cupid told Psyche severely. 'And far too curious.'

'What am I going to do?' she wept. 'I'll never be able to find my way back to your palace. Venus will only give me another impossible task to do.'

'Leave all this to me,' said Cupid. 'I shall talk to Jupiter.'

Following their discussion, Jupiter summoned Psyche, Cupid and Venus before him. He explained to Venus that all the tasks she had set Psyche had now been completed.

'Perhaps,' said Venus, still unrelenting, 'but she broke the rules. Don't forget that Psyche was told quite clearly that if she ever saw her lover she would die – and that's a prophecy that is yet to be fulfilled.'

Cupid tried to intervene on Psyche's behalf. 'I want to marry her,' he pleaded.

'There's only one way out of this,' proclaimed Jupiter. 'If Psyche forfeits her mortality and becomes a goddess, then she will have fulfilled the prophecy and I will agree to the marriage. But there is another condition. Cupid, the gods are tired of you continuously firing arrows at them. If you really want to marry Psyche, you must only fire arrows at humans.'

'When do I become immortal?' Psyche asked eagerly.

'Never – if I have my way,' retorted Venus bitterly.

But Jupiter's decision was final. He gave Psyche heavenly ambrosia to eat, and her mortality immediately dropped away. She and Cupid made their home on Mount Olympus, where Psyche bore a child called Pleasure.

People and Places in Roman Mythology

The stories in this book have a large cast of characters, and some only make a brief appearance. In other stories not included in this book, however, these characters have histories of their own. Some more information about them is included below, together with a brief description of some of the places where the stories occur.

AENEAS   The son of Anchises, the prince of Troy, and Venus, the goddess of love. He was destined to lead his people from the fall of the city of Troy to found a new and greater city in Italy. The story of his adventures was recorded by the Roman poet Virgil in his poem the *Aeneid*.

ALBA LONGA   A town in Italy, founded by the son of Aeneas in the Alban hills, about 20 kilometres from Rome.

CUPID   One of the beautiful children of Mars and Venus, mischievous Cupid was appointed god of love. He had wings and carried a bow and quiver of arrows. He was known to fire his arrows at gods and men. He used a gold-tipped arrow if he wanted them to fall in love, and a lead-tipped arrow if he wished them to repel it. According to Roman legend, he didn't grow up like a normal child. He remained small and chubby with rosy skin until his brother, the god of Passion, was born. From that moment he began to grow into a handsome, slender youth.

ETRUSCANS   People who lived on the west coast of Italy many years before the city of Rome was founded. They were very powerful, but after many battles they were defeated by the Romans in 300 BC.

ISLANDS OF THE BLESSED   The land given to the Titans by Jupiter when they had been conquered by the gods. They were believed to be in the far west of the universe, beyond the stars.

MARS   The god of war and son of Jupiter and Juno, the king and queen of the gods.

MERCURY   The son of Jupiter and the messenger of the gods. Mercury possessed a pair of winged sandals so he could carry out his tasks more quickly.

NEPTUNE   The brother of Jupiter and Pluto. Between them they ruled over Heaven (Jupiter), the sea (Neptune) and the Underworld (Pluto).

OLYMPUS   A mountain in northern Greece, believed to be the home of the gods. The Ancient Greeks, from whom the Romans adopted this belief, thought that this was the centre of the world.

PALATINE HILL/PALATINUS   One of the seven hills upon which Rome was built. The Roman emperor's palace was situated here, along with the homes of wealthy Romans.

RIVER TIBER   The river that runs through Rome, named after King Tiberinus of Alba Longa. When he drowned in its waters, Jupiter made him the god of the river.

SABINE PEOPLE   An ancient tribe who lived in the mountains east of Rome's River Tiber.

TITANS   Gigantic in stature, these were the first human beings to be created by Chaos, god of the unformed Earth. The gods and goddesses of Roman mythology were the children of the Titans.

VESTAL VIRGINS   Priestesses who tended the sacred fire in the temple dedicated to Vesta, goddess of the family hearth.

Index